This Book is Dedicated to Salaiah,

"I'm a Movement by myself, but I'm a Force when we're together Darling I'm good all by myself, but Baby You... You Make Me Better"

-FABOLOUS

LEVEL UP

TABLE OF CONTENTS

DISCLAIMER

The ideas expressed in this book are based off my own personal experiences and opinions. I am neither a licensed and certified Psychologist or Psychiatrist. That being said, much of the subject matter of this book involves deep psychological and emotional work and I strongly suggest seeking the help of a credentialed professional to help guide you to health and healing. None of the ideas or methodology in this book are meant to take the place of professional treatment. If you are in physical danger **PLEASE** contact your local authorities.

FOREWORD

FOREWORD

A full moon beamed down directly on to me through top of my bay window as I lay in the darkness. It seemed to stare directly at me. I couldn't sleep. Again. The girls had long since gone to bed but I found myself up well into the night unable to quiet my mind enough to fall asleep, per usual. I had a pretty standard set of dialogues that tended to occupy my mind during the night, most of which were psychic conversations between me and my youngest daughters father.

He and I had been friends in high school. We were considered some of the "smart kids", and met at an extracurricular club called Upward Bound. We bonded over a shared sense of not quite fitting in to the aesthetic of our hood surroundings. We attended different schools , but since we lived in the same neighborhood we would ride the bus together after the program and talk about any and everything. He is a few years younger than me so at that time it was pretty much unthinkable that anything could happen between us, at least in my mind, but I could tell he had a crush on me. I did think he was cute, but I believed that the boy should be older than the girl in a relationship and that was that on that.

Fast forward through graduation, a few kids and failed relationships later, and we became Facebook friends. We didn't interact that much online. He was just sort of in the periphery of my news feed, so I was vaguely familiar with the changes he had been going through since our high school days. We reconnected during the end of my on again/off again situationship with my oldest daughters father. I actually went through a mental breakdown during that time and was coming back to myself. He made a flirty comment on one of my pictures and I responded. From there we started communicating directly through messenger and eventually on the phone.

I had gotten pregnant with my oldest daughter at the end of my first semester in college and my self image was demolished as a result. I felt I had irreparably diminished my prospects and forfeited my dreams of a lifestyle somewhere between that of the characters Joan Clayton (of the TV show Girlfriends) and Carrie Bradshaw (of Sex and the City). I was perpetually depressed and dejected and was convinced that the best I could hope for was to get my (oldest) child's father to marry me and create for her the idyllic life that I myself never got to experience with my parents. I spent eight years on an emotional rollercoaster with the "frenemy" that was her father, a ride that crashed landed with me losing my mind, my home, and the fire that had driven me forward for all those years.

Crazy as it may seem, I came out of that situation with a sense that despite having lost "everything" I would be able to rebuild my life on a stronger foundation that was rooted in positivity instead of compulsion. So, when my second daughters father popped back into my life I took it as a good omen. Talking to him brought back many feelings I hadn't felt since high school. I'm not even talking about romantic feelings. I'm talking about the feeling of being young and expecting life to get better later. The feeling of anticipation of great things to come. I also remembered what it felt like to feel like my "intelligence" was something that made me special as opposed to weird. My oldest daughters father wasn't exactly an intellectual type, and we had had many an encounter where he perceived my sense of humor or tastes as bourgiose', and I hadn't realized how stifled I had been feeling up until then.

Our conversations were as long and multifaceted as they had been when we were younger. We discussed history, mythology, spiritualism, politics. My oldest daughter's father interest in me had been purely physical (at least that's how it felt) and that had been a deep source of hurt and shame for me. So when he (second BD) told me how much he had always admired my intelligence and that he knew I was destined for great things, then and now, It was like the balm my wounded soul needed. I finally had a Lover AND Friend in the same man.

My bliss was short lived, however. As I mentioned before, I was still dealing with the fallout of my breakdown (homelessness, joblessness) as well as my ongoing mental and emotional health issues. I was not in the position to be starting a new relationship as I had way more important things to be tending to. You may be of the mindset that there is nothing wrong with falling in love while you are down and out, but the reality is that if your priorities are askew you can wind up digging yourself deeper into the hole you are in if you are not careful, as I did. I was not focused or fully present in the realities of my life at that particular time and did not take the proper precautions as someone in my position should have. As a result I wound up pregnant, again.

His behavior in terms of our relationship had already been a bit sketchy to be totally honest. So I wasn't shocked when his inconsistency became less subtle after finding out about the pregnancy. Our friendship was more important to me than the romantic relationship though, and I tried to prevent things from getting to the point where I wanted nothing to do with him at all (having learned my lesson from the situation with my first baby daddy). I tried to let him off the hook, telling him that it was ok if he didn't want to be "with" me and that I would be happy raising this child with him as friends, but he insisted that he wanted our family and was committed to building that with me.

To make a long story short, he was full of shit. He wound up cheating on me a couple of times and I finally wised up and decided that I had no time to indulge in unnecessary drama, as I was about to become a single mother of two daughters. I "put on my big girl panties" and pushed through the rest of my pregnancy, making decisions for a family of 3 instead of 4. I was able to find a housing for me and the babies right after my youngest's first birthday. Housing that happened to be only two blocks away from her father, his new girlfriend, and *their* brand new baby.

Living so close to him, I felt, was a sign that we would find a way to raise our daughter together as friends if nothing else. I was as open and clear about my intentions as possible and I strived to keep my energy pure. Despite his attempts to maintain the possibility of a romance between us I intentionally kept our conversations limited to subject matter pertaining to the care and maintenance of our child. At this point in my life I had come to understand that interest doesn't equal investment, and was quick to point out to him that his words and actions weren't in sync and so were to be discounted. He had a whole new family after all.

I was proud of myself for how far I had come, yet I was still holding on to hope that he would "grow up" and decide to work towards getting me back. You see, while I was adamant that I would not let him make a fool of me again I still believed that he did in fact Love me. The way that he spoke of his current relationship, he hadn't intended for things to go this far and he had simply resigned himself to "bite the bullet" in order to do the "right" thing. The reality was that she, unlike me, had dug her heels in after their first child (of 3) and refused to "Allow him" (her words) to leave her just to do the same thing with someone else. He was just taking advantage of her determination not to be a single mother.

She paid all the bills while he was the babysitter (yes he considered himself such). She also felt entitled to dictate how he interacted with his children's mothers (he had two before me), more so out of her necessity to make sure he wasn't cheating than any warranted need. It was a messy situation, and while I strived to stay above the ratchetness of it all I still missed my friend, but would not allow myself to feel close to him as long as he was still trying to play both sides of the fence. He, in turn, would sneak behind her back to talk to his ex's when and how he wanted.

I lived in my apartment for about 3 years and during that time we had a few falling out periods of no contact because of his inconsistency towards our daughter, but there were a some months long stretches where things worked well and I would happily drop my daughter off to him and her to spend time with them and her siblings. I came to like her and was grateful for her kind treatment of my baby as evidenced by my daughters attachment to her. She and I would talk here and there and sometimes she would confide in me about his unfaithfulness and emotional abuse towards her. I would share what I had learned on my own journey about how the fear of single motherhood drove me to make concessions at the cost of my own wellbeing ,and assured her that I understood her choice to stay and supported her as a woman and mother.

That being said, I still held the belief that their relationship was built on dysfunction and that if he ever "got himself together" mentally, emotionally, and financially, that he would want to share his "best self" with me. I had become a reluctant yet benevolent middle man in their relationship, an accidental unpaid couples therapist for them while living my own life and raising my and his child pretty much on my own. I had begun an internal read of both him and her while I lay there, scolding them for being so oblivious to the discord they were creating and expecting me to think of them and their problems before my own. I caught myself mid rant and was fed up with them and MYSELF for having let this go on for so long. So there I was, alone in the dark, crying in the light of the full moon, begging God to remove this stupidity from my heart and life.

I was tired of feeling like I was waiting for my life to begin while both of my children's fathers had moved on and created whole new families. It was crazy to me that these people who had abandoned me AND their children and were able to find someone to Love THEM and fight to keep them while I couldn't. It was crazy to me that I had gotten that deeply involved with him and his new relationship that I hadn't even found the time to find one of my own. I realized that I had been isolating myself form the possibilities of the present by holding on to the past and begged God OUT LOUD and with all I had in me to take the idea that me and him could and SHOULD be together from my mind. I wanted to live MY life, the life that up until that point had only been going on AROUND me, to it's fullest. I was willing to give up the happily ever after I envisioned in order to receive the blessings available to me in the real world.

I cried and prayed, and prayed and cried until I felt empty. It honestly wasn't that long, not even a full 10 minutes. Then, I felt it wash over me, PEACE. I felt PEACEFUL! Full disclosure, I still felt like I was open to the idea of he and I getting back together IF and when he "got himself together". I just knew in that moment that I was done suffering because of what was or wasn't going on between me and my child's father. I also DECIDED that I wasn't going settle for less when dealing with new prospects because of the belief that this was just the "meantime in between time" before reconciling with him.

From that moment on, I viewed him, and the things that he did with a grain of salt. Unbothered doesn't even touch the level of apathy I have towards him to this day. I stopped any and all attempts at trying to make "fetch" happen. Unfortunately, this resulted in his disappearance from my daughters life altogether, but he honestly wasn't doing anything good while there anyway. The moment that the desire to be with him dissipated so did his leverage which meant that there was no longer any emotional payout for him.

An opportunist will always fall to the wayside once the opportunity is gone. I believe that someone who truly intends to do good for goods sake will continue to do so even when there is nothing for them to gain. It is my belief based on what I know about him and his history that my youngest daughters father is seeking the attention and unconditional love that he didn't get from his parent's, especially his mother as a child. As a result, he is continually seeking a maternal type of attention like the kind he got from me in our friendship. Once I realized that was what I had that he wanted I also was able to understand that it wasn't him that I was holding to, **but the feeling of being essential to him**. However, I want a man, not a son, and my daughter needs a father, not a brother.

Understanding the dynamics at play between us would never have been possible if I was still stuck in the paradigm of romantic love between he and I. I tried to make this story as concise as possible, so a lot of details have been left out, but my point is that I was putting myself through a bunch of mental and emotional gymnastics in order to justify continuing unnecessary and emotionally harmful contact with a person that was INCAPABLE of providing what I wanted from him, and that you, in your own way, are doing the same with your child's father.

The details may differ. His motivations may differ. For example, he may actually be a good and dutiful father but is stringing you along emotionally out of fear that you will try to keep him from his child. Or he could just be a man whore (shrugs). Despite the differences in our baby daddies however, I am confident that I know why you are participating in this cycle of drama. No matter what the underlying dynamic is, if you felt the need to open this book I assume you are not getting what you want and need out of the situation, and that you, **understanding that you are the only factor in this equation that you can control**, are seeking guidance as to how to move past this. So without further ado.....

LEVEL UP

INTRODUCTION

The new way of describing women moving past failed, toxic relationships is the term LEVELING UP. The music artist Ciara is the poster child for this phenomena, having swiftly secured the husband of **ALL** of our dreams, who is devoted, doting, handsome, rich, and committed to the her and their family, after making the all too common mistake of investing herself too much and too fast into the "Grand Poobah" of all fuckboys, Future. Her life is a testament and blueprint of how to win after losing so horribly and publicly. If only we all could manage to bounce back in such grand fashion, but alas, most of us must take a much longer, harder route to happiness.

I myself am an example of this. I have made the same mistake... **TWICE**... in terms of carrying children for men that didn't stick around to raise them with me. While I had learned my lesson enough with the first child's father so as not spend as long being dragged emotionally by the second child's father, I still felt badly that I wasn't careful and had dug myself even deeper into the hole that a lot of single mothers feel they are in. It is the *idea* of that hole that both encourages us to dig ourselves deeper by making even worse decisions, and/or prevents us from believing that we deserve the things that will come from making better decisions. I am here to tell you that you deserve all the best life has to offer.

It may seem like I'm trying to sell you a fairy tale because Ciara is rich and beautiful and connected in ways that we may never be able to compare to. But I know a secret that I'm going to share with you right now...and that secret is that *in order to receive a blessing, you must first let go of what you're holding on to*. More than likely the reason that you have yet to triumph over the situation between you and your child's father is because you are unwilling to let that situation go in a **real way**.

Sure, you may take "breaks". You may have "friends". You may "do you" any or all the time. However, in your mind the relationship between you and your child's father is **still** the end goal. In your mind everything and anything that may be going on right this moment means nothing in the grand scheme of things because at the end of your story it's you and him, together forever, living Happily. Ever. After. How are you going to have a Ciara Russell situation if you're still fully invested in your "Future"? You can't have it both ways. You're going to have to let something go and instead of it being the possibility your "Russell" why not let it be the sad, tiring reality of your "Future" so that you can have a *real* future that's worth having?

What you may not have realized is that your attachment to him actually has little to do with him. It has more to do with your relationship with yourself and the people that were responsible for you in your youth. Most of us that find

ourselves chasing Love in all the wrong places have some deep emotional need that we haven't fully explored. It is that need that drives the non-sensical behavior that has us out here looking crazy in these streets.

I want to make something crystal clear. This book is not a manual on how to get a man that's better than your baby's father. I mean that is one of the millions of options that you will be providing yourself by by severing the ties that bind you to him, but that **IS** not, and **SHOULD** not, be the end goal. My main motivation and putting these things down for distribution and consumption by women who come from where I've come from is to empower you to break free of any limiting mindsets, any guilt, any shame, any mental and emotional chain that **YOU** may be using to punish, sabotage, and torture yourself, and to make sure that you never, **EVER**, seek to destroy yourself using those or any other methods again. Not only that, I want to make sure that you are strengthened, capable, and focused on **raising the children that you happen to have summoned into this world** during your struggles so that they may pass on the legacy of you in your triumph as opposed to the pain of you in your diminished state.

A big hands off topic in our community (the Black Community) is the mental and emotional state of single parents, especially single mothers, and how it adversely affects their children.

Many of us will loudly profess the pain our mothers inflicted on us and yet can't make the correlation between the similarities in our romantic choices and how our children might be affected in similar ways to the ways we were. We **HAVE GOT** to be better. We have got to *DO* better, because we have more of an opportunity than ever to learn better. Maybe our parents didn't teach us. Maybe our community didn't care for us to know. But it is our duty to learn and do better for our children's sake. And, this book is meant to end of any and all deniability of culpability and alternatives, and usher in the beginning of a Golden Age for us all.

PART ONE: LIFTING THE "VEIL"

UNCOVERING THE HIDDEN MINDSET BEHIND YOUR ACTIONS

STEP ONE: LIFTING THE VEIL

The imagery of having the veil lifted from over your face has two meanings. One typically more preferred than the other. If you have trouble letting go of the idea of you and your child's father being a couple you more than likely have envisioned your own bridal veil being lifted to reveal you to him in all your splendor. In most cases it's this fantasy that is mechanizing the cycle of poor judgement and regret in which you find yourself stuck. In this instance the veil you don is one of delusion, wishful thinking, and projection.

I can remember instances with both of my children's fathers where I was faced with the proof of their disinterest in me and or my feelings/needs and instead of taking it at face value I took the liberty of constructing a narrative that explained their behavior in a way that allowed me to not only forgive it, but to dismiss it. An example of this is the way I viewed my oldest daughter's fathers sexual interest in me despite his non-committal attitude towards a relationship with me. I believed to my core that he was just resisting "growing up", a sentiment that I unironically would also attribute to my youngest's father.

 I rationalized that he was seeking out people and situations where he could feel free and unencumbered and that I was requiring him to be more mature and responsible than he wanted to be in that moment. To make matters worse, I figured it was only a matter of time until he would be ready to settle down, and that when he did I would be there to take my rightful place at his side. I was basically wasting my precious time waiting for him to get tired of "sowing his wild oats".

I suffered through endless embarrassment, both public and private, as well as confusion because I refused to accept the writing on the wall. I would minimize if not flat out ignore the elephant sized signs that pointed towards me needing to move on while simultaneously and obsessively using a flashlight, tweezers and microscope to find the nonexistent proof that I wasn't wasting my own time. One time while pregnant with my youngest I couldn't get in contact with her father, who was actually my fiancé at the time. I had been calling and texting him here and there for several hours. Eventually I began to feel that he wasn't just busy and I began to get scared.

I reached out to every contact of his I was aware of, from his mother to his case worker. I even contacted my uncle, a retired law enforcement officer, to see if he could find out if anybody fitting his description had been found, dead or alive. I could hear the skeptical pity in his voice as he explained the unlikelihood of him being in actual danger. Needless to say, he surfaced a few *agonizing* days later. He claimed he had *"lost his phone"* and had been staying at the house of one of his cousins, whom I hadn't met. And what did I do? I rationalized that *he was under tremendous stress and just wasn't handling it as well as he should.*

While technically true, that didn't negate the fact that I needed to keep my stress levels down for the baby's sake if not my own, and that if I couldn't depend on him to be reliable in my delicate state then I needed to establish boundaries for my own peace of mind. I'm ashamed to say that he would "lose his phone" at least two more times before I would be done with him. Although I played the fool for my youngest child's father a few times too many I have to say that I was nowhere near as invested in him as I was my oldest daughter's father. As I mentioned before, by the time I got pregnant with my youngest daughter I had been through the ringer with my oldest's dad, an experience that culminated in me quitting my job, losing my home, and almost being 302'ed by my family when she was 8.

Mind you, this was after YEARS of back and forth between he and I. There were times when I would just get tired of chasing him and go on about my business, but he would always seem to come back around just as I appeared to get him out of my system. I was woefully uninformed about the ways of men and believed his attraction to me had to run deep for him to keep coming back over and over. I know I certainly wouldn't keep reestablishing contact with someone I wasn't trying to be with. Especially not someone who came at my neck every time the way I would his when he would pop back up out of nowhere. There's one particular incident that will stay with me until the day I die.

When my oldest daughter had just turned 2 years old her father came and knocked on my grandmother's door. It was a few weeks after her birthday. I believe mine had passed as well, and I'm glad, because it would have been ruined if it hadn't. I brought our daughter outside to sit with him and I sat outside as well. I told myself this was because of her being so young and all, but that was a common excuse we single mothers use that I will explain later. Even though he had missed her birthday and hadn't seen her in months he was especially focused on me, or more specifically my apathetic attitude towards him. At that point I was reading the writing on the wall and had come to accept that he just wasn't interested in being her father in practice.

He apologized for having missed her birthday and was profusely campaigning to thaw my cold attitude towards him. I was generally uninterested in his appeals. He had a been consistently inconsistent her entire life to that point and I was emotionally drained and numb. He had recently moved back to our city and requested that I bring our daughter to visit him at his new apartment that upcoming weekend so that he could make it up to the both of us. As far as I was concerned he and I had no relationship and I wasn't interested in one, but I desperately wanted for my daughter the experience of a biological father that I never got. I wanted her to know what it was like to be adored and coveted by her father. Even though I was skeptical about whether or not he would follow through beyond that day it still felt good to have his attention on **us** for once.

That day came and I made sure that she *and* I looked pretty. We took the long bus ride across town to his apartment. It was an attic apartment in a charming cottage like house tucked away from the street back behind lots of deep green bushes with waxy leaves. It was surprisingly spacious with one large bedroom a reasonably sized living room, tiny little kitchen tucked off to the side and a small but functional bathroom done in all white with an old-fashioned claw-foot porcelain tub. It was really cute. We all settled in and sat on his bed and he put on movies and cartoons for the baby. At this point it was so long ago that I couldn't tell you specifically what all we talked about but I know that eventually I begin to relax and we were having a good time.

Back when I had first had the baby I had suggested that he go to massage therapy school because he already had a knack for it and I thought he could make a lot of money. He had taken my advice, but while he was attending he wound up meeting the woman who would become his third baby's mother (I was his second). He asked me to come into the living room so that he could show me his massage table. I knew this was a ploy to get me alone, but I was low-key geeked about it. Needless to say we had sex.

 At that point in my life I genuinely believed that people could be taken at their word. That HE could *despite* all my prior experience to the contrary. It didn't make sense to me that he would go through all of this trouble, coming all the way to my grandmother's house, to convince me to bring our daughter up there just to have a quick roll in the hay. Unfortunately for me that was exactly what he had done. Once we finished, we joined our daughter in the bedroom sitting on the bed watching television. This part of the conversation I remember almost verbatim. I was riding high on the afterglow of our activities in the rush of rekindled "love". I turned to him cheerfully and asked him "So how are we going to do this?"

 He looked at me with the same puzzled look that I would see so many times on our daughter's face. "What do you mean?", he said. "How are we going to do this?" I repeated. "Am I going to move in here, or are we going to work at getting a new place that's bigger?" The confusion on his face expanded. He drew his neck back, his eyes narrowed and his lips puckered. "Quianna....I'm in love with Tish." Tish (not her real name) was the woman he met at massage therapy school. For reasons I'll never understand, he went on to explain that she had been pregnant but got an abortion, as if that somehow clarified for me what he had done and why he had done it.

I've never felt an emotional pain like that. I've got to be honest, even talking about it still brings tears to my eyes. That experience for me was more than just a case of unrequited love, a big part of my innocence left me that day. Like I said, there are certain things that, until that moment, had never even occurred to me any person would do. I asked him what he meant. He repeated himself, but it made no more sense to me then as it did the first time it came out of his mouth. I asked him why he had bothered to do all of this? Why come my grandmother's house and campaign so heavily to get me up here if he was in love with another woman? His answer to this question was much simpler and clearer than the other. *"Because I like having sex with you."*

 The term rude awakening doesn't quite fit the severity of the impact of that moment on my psyche. Something broke in me, real rap. Although I felt like the wind had been knocked out of me I willed myself enough strength not to let him see me cry. I picked up my baby's diaper bag and left there with as much dignity as I could scrape from the bottom of my soul. That long bus ride home wasn't nearly long enough. My body felt weak and limp, but somehow I still managed to make it home. I can't remember what else I did the rest of that day.

All I remember is that evening, after preparing the baby for bed, laying down beside her in the dark, the pain swelling in the pit of my stomach and rising up through my chest and out of my mouth. I thought I did my best to stifle my sobs so as not to wake her but I don't think she was even sleep to begin with. My body was heaving with grief and devastation. Then, I felt a small soft hand oh my shoulder. In the dark my **two-year-old baby** turned me gently to her, reached out, wrapped her little arms around my neck, and held me to her chest. She made not one sound.

This act of pure love and nurturing so far beyond her years eroded what little pride and restraint I had left. She just held me there, in the dark, while I cried and cried for all I felt was lost to me that day. When I was all but delirious from both the events of the day and the sharp throbbing headache I get whenever I cry like that I regained my composure and took back the reigns of motherhood from my toddler. I scooped her into my arms and kissed her all over her face. Words couldn't express how proud, awed, grateful, and humbled I felt towards her in that moment. That day, I experienced both the greatest pain, and greatest Love I have ever experienced in my life.

Much later in life it became clear to me that all of that anguish and more could have been avoided. I wish that I could tell you that was the moment I decided to leave my daughters father alone for good, but it wasn't. As time passed and I put the agony and embarrassment I felt behind me. I focused on my life and continued to navigate improving myself and my situation without him. I had good friends and the occasional lover. But, the desire to be a family *with **him***, as well as the belief that it was possible hadn't left me.

Single motherhood can be isolating, especially when you try not to have a revolving door of boyfriends around your child. I had grown up feeling like my mother had prioritized having a man over building a relationship with me, so at a very young age I vowed that I would never do that to my child if I ever had one. I had never learned how to vet men or how to be a proper steward of my sexuality so as to get the pleasure I was seeking while not further feeding my deep seated emotional wounds. I was living a kind of double life that was depleting me mentally and emotionally. What I truly craved was to be loved and prioritized in the way neither of my parents had done. But I was also in my 20's and wanted to fuck. So I settled for friends with benefits, or in the case of my daughters father, a frenemy with benefits.

One of my most deep running false beliefs was that the sexual chemistry between us was the *proof in pudding* that he Loved me. It made no sense that he would go months at a time with no contact between us (this includes contact with his daughter), would have girlfriends, more children, live a whole life apart from me and our child but always manage to show up at my doorstep with just as much passion and desire as he had when we first met. I can't lie, the sex was AMAZING. No one knew how to make me tingle like him. No one was as sensual. No one was as dedicated to pleasing me (physically). Aw Hell, I'm just gonna say it, NO ONE COULD BEAT AND EAT LIKE HIM *shrugs*. I would let go of all my inhibitions when we would have sex. I felt strong and powerful, and in control while at the same time feeling surrounded and protected and dominated by him. Knowing what I know now, I understand that I felt truly **FEMININE** when we had sex and it was intoxicating (put a pin in that for later).

I couldn't imagine anyone else being able to do to my body what he did. Combine that with the fact that he was the father of my only child (at that time) as well as my emotional baggage from my childhood (mommy AND daddy issues, identity issues) then mix in the guilt I felt for having gotten pregnant in the first place, diminished self esteem, anger at the sacrifices I and ONLY I was making for our child, I could go on... and this was an emotional and mental environment ripe for the kind of obsession and delusion I exhibited for all those years. I had my moments of clarity (when he ghosted) where I would forget all about him (or so I thought) and live for me and my daughter. I would make great strides in my personal development, setting and accomplishing goals. However, in the back of my mind there was always this idea that I was only doing this *in the meantime,* and that, one day, he would "wake up", or "grow up", and understand that I was the woman he needed by his side to conquer the world and fully actualize in the real world as the same "god-king" who owned me in the bedroom.

In short, *I* romanticized the dynamic between us into a timeless love affair for the ages that would inevitably end with us old and gray, looking back on the foolishness of our youth and the futility of our attempts at denying our true destiny of raising a family and building a Legacy, TOGETHER. The reality, however, was much less mythic. I bought in to the concept of *"THE BOND"*. I'm sure you're familiar with **The Bond**. It's the driving force behind so many single mothers crazy behavior when it comes to their baby's father. They will stalk, threaten, assault, damage property, and traumatize their OWN children in the name of their "right's" as *HIS Child's Mother.*

The Bond is the "veil" that you must lift from your face in order to excercise the control over your actions required to shape your reality with intention. The bond is distraction. The bond is delusion. The bond is drama. The bond is escape. We use the bond to justify nonsensical behavior and irresponsibility. That's right, you are being irresponsible by not establishing and maintaining proper boundaries with your child's father. Hurt feelings and petty arguments ultimately hurt the child(ren) more than the adults involved and are easily avoided when the lanes of all parties are clear and everyone stays in them. Lifting the veil is not about rehashing what he's done to you, it's about acknowledging what *you* didn't do to prevent it, taking accountability for that, forgiving yourself, and being proactive about preventing it in the future.

So how is this step achieved?

1. **Recognizing that having a baby for a man does not automatically make you his True Love. Or vice versa. Babies are a result of a biological process, sex. If the Love wasn't real or solid when the sex happened the resulting child isn't going to change that.**

2. **Admitting to yourself that you are not a victim in this situation and that what you are experiencing has more to do with who YOU are and what YOU have/haven't done than it does him and his actions.**

3. **A willingness to "be wrong". Throughout all of the arguments and drama you stand firm in the knowledge of your "righteousness". YOU"RE the good parent that does everything no matter what while he does what he wants when he wants. YOU"RE the loyal one, who thinks of his feelings in all you do while he shows yours no regard. YOU'RE the ride or die friend who's always there willing to see the best in him and give him another chance to get it right while he is distrustful and untrustworthy, constantly leaving you out to dry.**

One of the foundational components of the veil is the belief that not only are you *not wrong* for continuing this toxic dynamic with your child's father, but that you are **NOBLE** for doing so. That by making these "sacrifices" you are demonstrating **your** maturity, **your** loyalty, **your** unquestionable worthiness, making *him* the ungrateful and underserving villain, and *you* the victim of his selfishness and your own kind heart and loyal nature. So, since you are unable to rest assured in the relationship, you dig your heels into the position of being the one who is "**RIGHT**". There's just one problem. You're not *HAPPY*, Sis.

It is this sense of righteousness that will have you willfully wasting your own time and energy trying to control everything and everyone but yourself and wondering why your life is in shambles. **You**, who stays fighting him, his girlfriend, his MOMMA, you think **THIS** is RIGHT? Or, maybe you are the passive type, allowing him to play house with you when he is bored or can't be where he really wants to be. You think it's *RIGHT* to **ALLOW** him to treat you and your kid's like the second string? The change you seek by reading this book will come when you allow yourself to step outside yourself and take a sober look at your actions to this point.

What would you tell a friend that was acting the way you've been. What would you **THINK** but maybe not say? Exactly.

You're not truly ready to let go of your BF unless you are willing to take on all of the blame you've been projecting on to him for the way things have turned out. Not to beat yourself down with it, but to process it, to break it down so that you can let go of it and the negativity tied to it. There's a song that captures this vibe perfectly by Chrisette Michele that goes "blame it on me...say its my fault...as long as it's over..." .

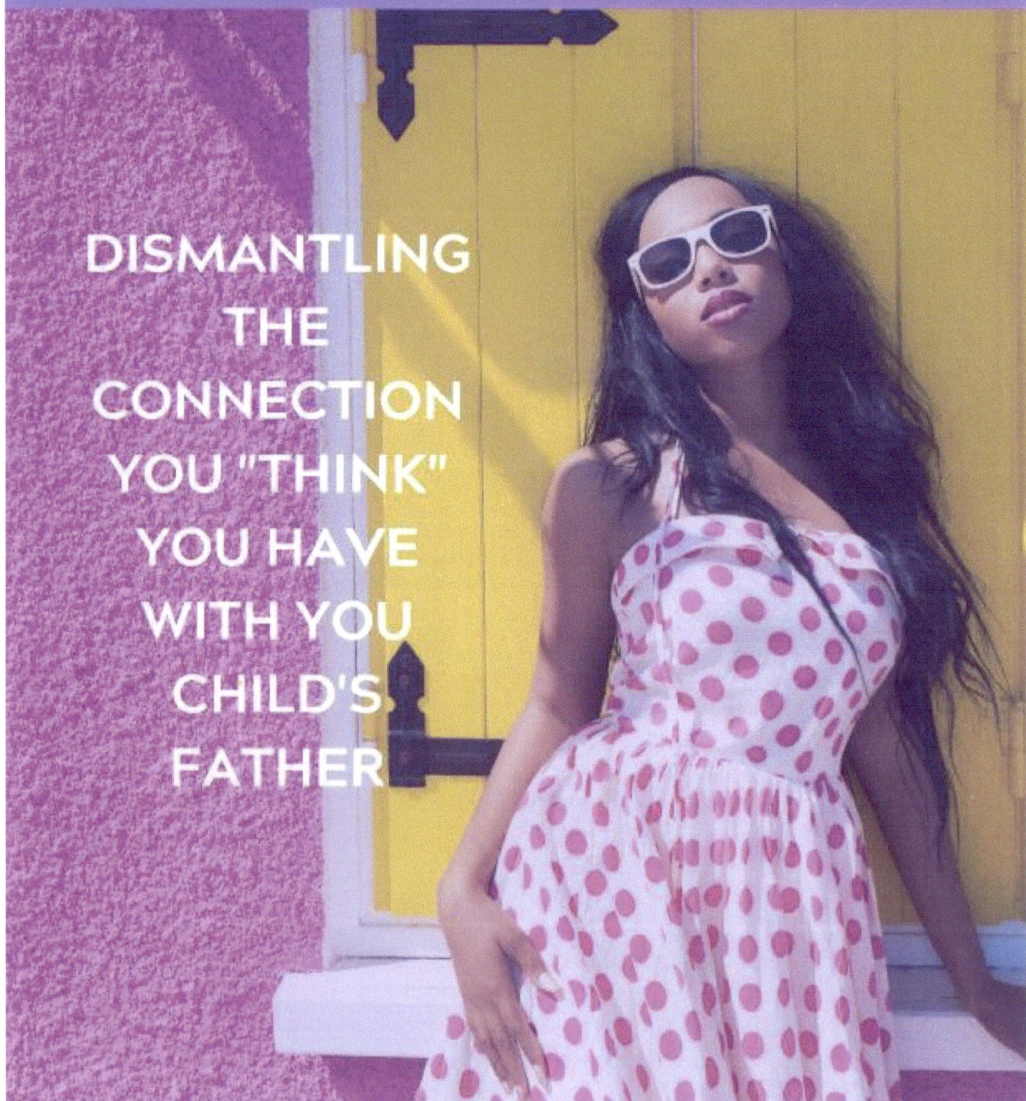

PART TWO: THE "BOND"

DISMANTLING
THE
CONNECTION
YOU "THINK"
YOU HAVE
WITH YOU
CHILD'S
FATHER

LEVEL UP

STEP TWO: DISMANTLE "THE BOND"

The BOND will have you so confused as to how your BF would prioritize anyone and anything over your desires when you are the obvious Love of his life. The BOND keeps you in a perpetual state of righteous indignation at the perceived dismissal of your feelings by him and everyone else in the entire world despite the fact that he is not your man, might even have a new woman, and never really prioritized your wishes when/if you were together in the first place. The BOND will have you thinking that you have any say at all on how he lives his life and conducts his relationships despite his every demonstration to the contrary. The BOND will have you making enemies out of other women and wasting your energy trying to keep them from enjoying what you covet. But the most diabolical function of THE BOND, however, is providing yourself an excuse for continued sexual contact with your BF.

I believed in the Bond between myself and both of my children's father's but I have to say that my fixation on my oldest daughters father was the most destructive. As I mentioned before we had a strong sexual chemistry and I wanted so badly to believe that it meant something more. The reality though was that he and I had unprotected (albiet PHENOMENAL) sex that resulted in the conception and birth of a child that neither one of us wanted at the time or was prepared to care for, and that *I* couldn't justify having an abortion *within my own mind*, so I had her, and was trying **desperately** not to have to raise her alone. I know. It seems cold. Maybe even cruel. It definitely doesn't seem like something a loving mother would say about the way her *God given gift* of a baby got here, but it's the truth. The simple, **UN FILTERED** truth.

The saying goes *"The Truth is a hard pill to swallow"*. The validity of this saying is heavily apparent in the way single mothers feel the need to mask the pain, shame, embarrassment, **regret**, and fear of not only what may happen, but also of what they may have FORFIETED by having their child(ren) (freedom, baggage free dating, the perfect family image) by constantly and DEFENSIVELY insisting how much they love their kid(s) and how much of a blessing they are when they feel *those kinds* of truths creeping close. Single mothers cling to the bond in hopes that their worst fears are just that (fears) and they won't have to face the uncertainty that lies behind them.

As a single mother it can be easy to get lost in the idea that in order to give your child the best life you have to include their father, but if the father is not including **himself** you shouldn't be towing his line. I personally struggled with doing the most in order to provide my child with a nuclear family structure but all I succeeded in doing was creating chaos and building the foundation of dysfunction in the formative years of my oldest daughter's life. I wanted a shortcut. I wanted to be able to relax in the knowledge that the only man around my daughter was her father so that I didn't have to worry about things such as pedophilia or other types of abuse that could have been a factor with an unrelated man.

However, her father proved to be just as disruptive if not more so in our lives despite what I felt was his inherent connection to my daughter. He was not prioritizing her the way I would have expected considering he was her biological parent. In some ways he was even more dismissive because he was so sure that the fact that she was his biological child was enough. Not to mention that his primary focus seemed to be maintaining enough of a relationship with me to use me at his leisure as opposed to secure and contribute to a solid environment and emotional foundation for his child.

The quickest way from point A to point b is a straight line. The zig zags swoops and swirls of you and your BF's relationship trajectory is a definitive indication of its fixed path to nowhere. I won't presume to say that once a man's mind is made up about you it can't be changed, but I can say with all certainty that it is a fools errand to spend your time trying to change it. Doing so will steadily erode your confidence, deplete your self-esteem, and block any Joy you could experience, leaving you a shell of the woman you once were and could be. That is no way to live, and your children deserve a better mother than that.

So how do you fix it? First, you must let go of the belief that the relationship between you and your baby's father is viable and has a fruitful future. I consider myself reasonably optimistic and so when I was doing the work of mentally and emotionally separating myself from these types of desires I told myself that it was totally possible that One day, me and my child's father could find ourselves back in each other's arms, healthy and whole, committed and secure. However in **this** moment that is not the case and it doesn't serve me, or more importantly my child, to devote any more of my energy to TRYING or WAITING for it to happen. Then and there I committed to diverting no more of my precious life force to that endeavor.

I made a promise to myself, my children, and my God to no longer squander the gift of every moment allowed me by my creator focusing on things that brought me anything but joy, improvement, or affirmation. Love can be sacrificial at times but it should not hurt more than it heals. With these things as my foundational paradigm it became crystal clear what was right for me to do, both morally and as the leader in my own life. You don't really believe that he's the only one for you. **You just don't believe anyone else will want you**. You think he's your only option and so you're willing to let him drag you through the mud just so that you don't have to be alone.

Tony Robbins said "Change happens when the pain of staying the same is greater than the pain of change". I had hit an emotional wall and couldn't stand feeling that way anymore. I was to the point that I didn't care if I was alone for the rest of my life, but I was not going to feel that way a minute longer. If you're willing to accept anything just so you don't get what you perceive to be nothing you will always lose. You have to believe me, I know firsthand. So how do you manage to live your best life and achieve the Omarion level of unbothered-ness? You turn inward. You face your fears. You're a parent so I'm going to assume you've at least heard of the movie FROZEN if not seen it a million times. On the off chance that you have not I'll provide a brief explanation.

The main character, Elsa, has a power that she views as a curse after making a mistake and hurting her younger sister accidentally. From then on she spends most of her time and energy trying to hide and suppress it. As a result, her power grows and overwhelms her and her whole kingdom and she runs away. She winds up almost actually killing her sister (again by accident) until she realizes that if she focuses on the Love she feels instead of her fears that she is able to control her powers and undo the damage she's caused. Much like Elsa, it is the fear of the consequences of our actions that causes us to act impulsively, digging ourselves deeper and deeper in and further isolating us from what we truly want. We expect the Love needed to regain control and free ourselves to come from others when it is really our own Love and attention that will set us free.

Elsa's overarching fear was that she would hurt the one's she loved most. So in order to prevent that, she literally kept herself away from them, locking herself in her room and eventually running off into the mountains. It never occurred to her that embracing herself and letting herself relax and enjoy the way she felt about her loved ones would help her control her power better, eliminating the need to protect them against it. Like Elsa, I was so focused on preventing what I feared that it caused me to suffer through my life experience instead of allowing myself to enjoy my blessings.

After many years of reflection, soul searching, and unabashed honesty **with** myself **about** myself, I've come to the understanding that my actions during the first 8 years of my oldest daughters life were driven by:

1. The *Womanly* fear that I had permanently handicapped myself in the dating market if not disqualified myself outright by becoming a single mother

2. The *Childhood* fear of causing my child to feel like I valued a man's presence my life over hers

My self-worth was damaged by the pain and shame of getting pregnant under those circumstances and I had put myself under tremendous stress and pressure to live up to the standard of motherhood I felt my own mother had failed to afford me. This triggered in me an obsessive need to redeem my value as a woman by getting my daughters father to marry me, simultaneously achieving my goals of properly prioritizing her and her needs and satisfying my own carnal desires without having to sleep around. The result, however, was me rationalizing letting my daughters father and other men use me as a living sex doll, using unprotected sex as a substitution for emotional intimacy, and idealizing my relationship with him as some cosmic event instead of the bad decision it was for years to come.

What buried fears are you fighting against in your own life?

What makes you feel icky or ashamed about your circumstances?

What disappointments did you experience in your past that shape how you try to act in the present?

What are you afraid you might have cost yourself by having your child(ren)?

The answers to these questions are a perfect place to start your introspection process. The things you have been doing up until now have been driven by these underlying factors. These are your "strings" or "buttons".

Fully understanding what makes you tick will give you insight on how/why you tend to be so gullible when it comes to your child's father, and maybe other people as well. It will also help you to clarify your intentions making it possible for you to frame your intentions in the positive instead of in the negative. I'll give you an example. I felt that I would only attract low quality men because I was "damaged goods" and had "baggage", so I assumed that my best bet was to not waste my time trying to get anything but dick from men other than my daughters father while waiting for him (the father of my child) to decide to marry me because he should already have had a vested interest in my child. But that kept me extremely limited, as opposed to me ***setting the intention*** of putting myself in the best position possible to attract a kind and caring man that would embrace both me and my child emotionally.

One mind set is RE-active while the other is PRO-active. Investigating and then facing your own fears will give you the necessary insight to begin to make decisions instead of concessions. Once you are able to clearly understand why it is you have been doing what you do and allowing what you have you will have exposed your hidden drives, eliminating your need to keep using THE BOND as an excuse to stay stuck on stupid. You will be able to clearly identify the patterns in your life and make the needed adjustments. This knowledge will be a game changer.

As single mothers we are constantly bracing ourselves against the harshness of disappointment and the judgements of others. You will need to make a conscious decision to make the time to do this emotional work and take the proper precautions. You will be vulnerable during this time. This is a time where you will be identifying your needs, clarifying your desires and establishing the boundaries needed to meet and acquire them. It's a time of getting to know yourself all over again. It's a time of nurturing yourself. Of falling in Love with yourself. You are building structure where there was none and must be careful not to let yourself be influenced by anyone who benefits more from you staying the same.

PART THREE: LEVELING UP

MAKING THE MOST OF YOUR NEWFOUND FREEDOM AND OPPORTUNITIES

STEP THREE: CUT OFF ALL UNNECESSARY CONTACT

Baby fathers are the biggest beneficiaries of the concept of the bond. It affords them the security of a preferential position in our lives as well as the prerogative to maintain their autonomy. I don't consider either one of my children's father's friends of mine. I believe that friends do what they can to help you through tough situations, especially situations they helped create. And if they can't help, the least a TRUE friend would do is take care not to make matters worse. I came to realize over time that if neither one of my baby's fathers were going to share in the responsibility for the care and upkeep of their respective children OR set/respect the emotional and physical boundaries necessary to keep things running smoothly between us for our child's sake that they simply weren't to be trusted with the title of friend and the influence/benefits it bestowed.

It's important to note however that all of the responsibility doesn't fall on him. It is common in modern co-parenting relationships for the mother to presume that the father's efforts or willingness to maintain sexual contact with them is an indication of a deeper connection. We as women will go through painstaking lengths to justify having sex with our baby's father, lying to ourselves and causing ourselves tremendous amounts of stress and heartache. In some cases the man isn't even worth it! He doesn't take care of the child, emotionally or financially, he's selfish, stingy, entitled and possessive. He's more worried about keeping a new man out of your life than he is about being the man in his child's.

To be fair, Not all men are dead beats when it comes to their children. Some men, while fantastic fathers, still manage to be assholes when it comes to the mother. They might show up on time, provide financially, be steadfast and consistent where the kids are concerned. But he can still take advantage of your unrequited love. No matter how good of a father he may be, he is still a man, and **he will sleep with you and keep it moving if that is an option**, unless he has *exceptionally* high moral character. Sex does not always equal Love and you need to get real with yourself about what is actually going on between you. If he is the type of man you can respect as a father to your children don't jeopardize your rapport by putting him in a position to break your heart.

We women love to pass the buck, attributing the complications in our love lives to the men who "just won't let us go". This is bullshit and it's time to grow up and assume control of our behavior by taking responsibility for our own actions. People can only treat you how you allow them to. Furthermore, just because someone wants you doesn't mean you have to hand yourself over. There's some dude somewhere that's been waiting forever for you to give him a chance and the only reason he may come to mind right now is because I brought him up, so it's possible for a man to want you and for you to leave it right at that so let's please be done with the middle school mindset of not being able to escape the grips of a man's desire for us. The issue is that *YOU* want HIM and he is just ACCEPTING you on his own terms.

I'm a subscriber to the belief that what is meant for you will find it's way back to you if you let it go. If he's not staying put he's pulling away, so let him go. If he's not ready to commit that means he's not absolutely sure. If you have been being genuine with him about who you are and what you have to offer there's literally nothing more you can or should do. Sleeping with him out of laziness or to keep him close is a recipe for disaster. It's only a matter of time before things get messy. If he's not trying to really be with you than he's for the streets and you'd do well to remember that to avoid drama. Parents who are true platonic friends are better for the children than parents who are in a situationship.

FAMILY TIES

One of the most common lies that we tell ourselves on the subject of our children's fathers is that having sex or even just spending time with them **OUTSIDE OF WHAT IS ABSOLUTELY NECESSARY** is not only healthy, but *preferable* to meeting (and actually DATING) new people. We rationalize these situationships by categorizing what happens within them as "CO-PARENTING", a term that has come to be the single parents equivalent of "Netflix and Chill". That term is like nails on a chalkboard to me at this point because of its subliminal indication of *fuckery afoot* more often than not.

It is impractical to expect to spend holidays, take vacations, and spend all of your mutual free time with your BF if you two are not in a committed relationship. Is it POSSIBLE to build the kind of rapport between you that would make this type of scenario possible? Of course! But the likelihood of it being anything but a disaster is extremely low if you two are using these instances as an opportunity to carry on an illicit affair. ESPECIALLY if one or both of you have new love interests. Not only that, it puts the child(ren) in an volatile situation. It is confusing and cruel to have them in the middle of a love triangle, square, or maybe even a circle (there's something new every day chile).

Most kids would rather have their parents "be together" and giving them that experience here and there just to pull the rug from under them and be with your new boo on the regular and/or knowing they will have to be around his woman/your man is unfair and tacky. How are you supposed to teach them general respect for themselves and others when the both of you are disrespecting yourselves, her/him, AND them (the children) carrying on this way? Our children are learning both directly and indirectly from our actions. Even if you think you are keeping things under wraps children are sharp and pick up on more than you think.

LET'S TALK ABOUT SEX

Children are not benefited by your late night rendezvous with their father. Let me repeat that a little louder: **CHILDREN ARE NOT BENEFITTED BY YOUR LATE NIGHT RENDEZVOUZ WITH THEIR FATHER**. Nor do they benefit from conversations centered on sexual subject matter. I used to subscribe to the chain of thought that said that my baby fathers popping in and out and then back in again meant that he was emotionally tethered to me. In my own mind I believed that he wouldn't bother to continuously re-establish a connection with me unless I actually meant something to him.

I told myself that he was simply too immature and scared to admit to both me and himself that he wanted our family just like I did. I knew nothing of men, LOL. In retrospect, he would tell me the truth not just by his actions but in words as well. Sometimes I would ask him why he wouldn't just leave me alone, to which he would reply that **he enjoyed having sex with me and didn't want to stop**. Although sometimes I would sober up enough to accept that he was not going to be with me in the way that I wanted him to be, that meant no nookie for him and that was not something he was willing to accept. So he would turn his focus on me long enough to convince me (based on whatever my standard was at the time) so that I would acquiesce to his desires.

It can feel like you and your baby's father are destined to be together when all is said and done. All of the passion and drama can make it seem like you two I just star crossed lovers paying karmic dues in order to earn the blissful Nirvana of each other's consistent love. That's not true. The child you share is not a personification of your shared fate in deep love. **They are a bookmark to him.** They are the equivalent of a dogs quick spray of urine to Mark its territory (no offense to the baby). And unfortunately, in some instances they mean just as much (little) to him.

"It's not like that.. he loves our child". In his own way, yes. he might, but **what is the fruit of that love**? How does he express it? Does it bring comfort in the affirmation, or does it bring anxiety, insecurities, and chaos? Does he treat you like someone whose presence in his life he cherishes? Or does he treat you like a toy he is bored with but doesn't want anyone else to have? Most important of all does he take his responsibilities as a father seriously, and treat his children as entity separate from you and your failed romantic relationship, or does he treat them as an ever-present placeholder, his hand stamp for perpetual access through the Velvet rope of *"Club Puss"*?

As intoxicating as the idea of the "perfect family" can be, you must keep a sober enough mind to be both an advocate and protector of your children's psyche, as well as your own.

Children are highly intuitive and do not benefit from the impersonation of prioritization. They know it ain't about them, sis. Someone has to be the adult. And since you are the only one (I assume) putting in the time and effort to shape their world on a daily basis you're going to have to be strong enough and disciplined enough to reject the distraction and disruption of their fathers selfish exploitation of both you and them. You also need to take care not to lose your child's trust and respect by demonstrating a lack of good judgement in prioritizing the desires of your inner child over their (your child's) actual needs.

Instead of classifying your baby fathers intentions as good or bad look at it through the scope of whether or not you feel safe or unsafe, whether or not you feel secure or insecure, whether you feel supported or exploited. As I mentioned before, even men who are technically "good" will use you for sex if you're offering it as an option. It can feel like they are sending mixed signals but their intent is usually crystal clear. They just want to fuck you when it's convenient. Unfortunately for you, they aren't thinking about the long term effects it will have on your emotional health. But why should they if YOU'RE not?

You may think that his love for you would prevent him from doing things that would break you down. He has no love for you or at least know not your definition of love. His love is circumstantial and conditional upon the ease with which he can manipulate you. I do not say these things lightly. It is not my intention to poison your mind against men, however these are facts. These are THE facts.

They don't change because they may hurt your feelings. you must learn to control your feelings and not let your feelings control you because as long as your feelings control you all **he** has to do is control your feelings. You tell him things because you want to be close to him and he will use them to maneuver you the same way a puppeteer maneuvers a marionette. You may think that because you yell and scream and give ultimatums and fight and cry and cause a ruckus that you are deterring him in some way. That couldn't be farther from the truth.

 My oldest daughter used to get in so much trouble all of the time. People would think that I didn't punish her but that wasn't true. I would punish her all the time. I would spank her. I would take things from her. Anything that I could think of to try to get it through her brain that this behavior was not acceptable and yet she still persisted. As she got older I began to fear that I had absolutely no control as a parent over how she would act. One day I flat-out asked her if she even cared about the punishments. She told me that even though she didn't like the punishment she felt like they were temporary and that is long as she got what she wanted, in the grand scheme of things, they were a small price to pay.

 Now the relationship between a mother and a daughter is quite different than the relationship between a man and a woman. However between any two people once the dynamic is **set** it's the cycle in which the relationship will run. Your BF doesn't care so much about what the "consequences" are, only the **inevitable** reward. **The only real thing you could ever take from him is access to whatever it is that he seeks through his relationship with you**. Sex, money, shelter, or just plain old attention. In the interest of saving time let's just call these things *resources*. Whatever it is that he values in the situation, it surely isn't your state of mind or well-being. That much should be evident.

Someone has to be the grown-up. How is it that you can complain about this man about his immaturity about his selfishness about how he doesn't help or even put himself in a position to be able to help and yet still entertain the thought of letting him penetrate you? What sense does that make? Bottom line if the desire to provide, protect, and model good behavior for his own children is not enough to drive him in positive and fruitful pursuits then he is not a good or competent father and should not hold a position of power, dominance, leadership, or influence in your or your child's life. And on the flip side of the same coin, if he is a competent father but still chooses string you along you have to be an advocate for your own well being.

The very least he could do in the best interest of your child is to leave you alone in order that you can have a clear, focused mind and Spirit to better care for your child as a single parent. The fact that his main and probably only priority is keeping unfettered access to your vagina speaks volumes. Is there a chance that I am wrong? Of course! I believe that there is always a chance that whatever negative scenario you may be thinking is going on could be the complete opposite of the reality of the situation. But it's just as important if not more important to be open to the **possibility** of the most negative reality. It is the outright and full out denial of even the *slightest* possibility that your worst fears could be true that keeps you stuck in the situation. You must understand that just because you want something to be does not mean that it is.

You continuously ignore all the signals of a full-out wreck coming up fast on this road you've chosen to travel because you are convinced that your destination is happily ever after with this one person and no one else. This is a planet of billions of people! Surely someone out there could be better to and for you and your children. No one knows better than I the innumerable fears surrounding the idea of dating as a single mother. My stomach would churn at the thought of my child being hurt by someone brought into their life intentionally by me. I wouldn't be able to live with myself if my children were ever raped or otherwise abused by a man I insisted on having around them. A man that was there primarily for my own comfort and pleasure.

No mother wants to be the root cause of any trauma to their baby. But what you may not have considered is that you are inflicting all kinds of traumas and dysfunctional behavior patterns into your child through **your personal** interactions with their selfish and uninterested father. I want to reiterate that I do not believe that this is the case in all co-parenting situations, but sis you know if I'm talking to you or not. If your child's father can't be bothered to be involved and invested in the day-to-day ins-and-outs of their child's life that is unmistakably apparent. You know whether or not their status as father of the year exist in reality or just inside your hopes and dreams. You know whether or not the bond between your child and their father is built on quality time and paternal structure or solely on *your promotion* of him as such. Is his focus on them based on their need... or his leisure? Right, so you need to stop having sex with him. PERIODT. Thank You for coming to my TED talk.

So how do I expect you to tackle what might be the most difficult part of this entire process?

1. NO CONTACT AFTER YOUR CHILDS BEDTIME

There's nothing he may want to discuss that can't be done during daylight hours. He knows his child isn't up at 12:15 am. The only reason he would be calling at that time of night is to get up in your ear and then your guts. If you make a habit of bussing it up with him during booty call hours actual booty calls are not far off. "But what if its an emergency?" If the baby is with you then whatever he wants can wait until the next day. Let him leave a message or send a text. If the baby is with him answer, but if your child is not in distress let him know you'll contact him about it tomorrow.

2. CONDUCT YOUR CORRESPONDENCE THROUGH TEXT PRIMARILY

This is an especially good idea if you have an antagonistic relationship. This way everything is literally spelled out between you two. As an added bonus, if he tends to be disrespectful you will have proof handy should the authorities have to get involved. You will also be forced to control the way you speak to him as well since there will be "paper trail". This should help motivate you to not

compromise yourself by saying things you wouldn't want any record of.

3. **IF AND WHEN YOU CANNOT AVOID TALKING TO HIM KEEP IT SHORT AND CONCISE**
You don't need to know how he's been doing. It's none of his business if your still dealing with "dude". Even if you do miss him that is not an appropriate conversation for the two of you to be having. The only things that should be being discussed is the child's needs, schedule, and the particulars of any hand-off's or pick-up's. Other than that you need to be too busy for chit chat. You don't have to be rude about it. Just make it clear that your time is limited and behave accordingly. To be clear this has always been the case, limiting his access in this way just prevents you from wasting time and sets the tone for how *you* are WILLING to interact moving forward.

4. **REQUIRE THAT HE TAKE HIS CHILD(REN) OUT WHEN COMING TO VISIT THEM**
This isn't about him spending money. He should have a safe place to take his child(ren) when he wants to spend time with them instead of sitting up under you at your house. He can take them to his own house,

the park, his Momma's house, wherever he wants, he just can't be all up in your space. If you object to this on the grounds of your child's safety I suggest you hop back in to the section about "the veil". If you feel you can't trust the father of your child with their safety in your absence something is amiss and you need to reevaluate your intentions. Either he's a good (enough) father and you want to be with him if possible OR he's crazy and/or dangerous and if that's the case the last place he should be is in your house or bed Sis. Pick a struggle. If he objects on the grounds that he is only stopping by, offer to schedule another day when he has more time. Ask him what day works best for him. He should be willing to make the arrangements. If he's mad he will threaten to take you to court for visitation which shouldn't be a problem because you'll be getting what you want in the long run anyway. And if he's just full of shit he will bitch and complain but do nothing.

LEVEL UP

TRUST AND RESPECT

You can never truly love a man if you do not respect him. We tend to think that just because we want to be with someone it means that we love them but if you take the time to look at your reasoning for wanting to be with them you realize it has little or nothing to do with who they actually are as a person. Think about it you're always complaining about them you don't think today care enough about you or your children so what is the big draw? This is one of the biggest ways we sabotage ourselves when it comes to relationships is believing the ends will justify the means in the long run. All were doing is making ourselves suffer and dragging our babies down that long painful road with us.

The dynamic between my daughter's father and I was very adversarial. When we weren't having sex we were either arguing or not in contact. He would try to give me instruction all the time. In retrospect I believe that what he was seeking was a traditional male lead dynamic between the two of us. However, I would fight him at every turn even sometimes when he would be giving sound advice. Why was that? Because I didn't trust him! Why would I let someone I didn't trust give me counsel?

We do not trust nor respect these men. In some cases they don't work. They don't prioritize their own children. They lie.

You name it and they've done it. We have no respect for them. Yet still we want them to stay in our lives and play a major role???? But the silliest part about it was that even though I didn't trust him in general **I still wanted to be with him**. Make that make sense! If there is no trust between you and your child's father and there can't be anything good. When you don't trust them you'll always be wondering if what they say is meant to hurt you or help you.

We as women confuse our *desire* to trust someone as actual trust for them. We operate in a perpetual state of cognitive dissonance, fixating on any and every detail of the situation **except** the ones that glaringly support our least wanted outcome. You nag him about cheating. You berate him about being dismissive of your feelings. You defame him and his character to anyone and everyone who will listen, and yet you refuse to do the most logical thing, which is to leave him alone. You complain day in and day out about how unhappy you are how horrible of a partner he is and how he just won't leave you alone but the fact of the matter is he doesn't have to.

These men will use your emotions against you. They want you to love them as deeply as possible because they know that if you are in love with them there is no transgression too far out of bounds. They rely on that love to give them leverage. And with that leverage there is no reason to modify their behavior to suit your needs or desires. You are nothing but a resource to them. Being their baby's mother entitles them to a lifetime of emotional and/or financial support, shelter and/or food, and yes, sex. These men believe that impregnating you has marked you and that you will be accessible to them for the rest of your lives. And unfortunately, the way things have gone, this has been true in many cases.

Because of our own insecurities about how the world and how men may view us we accept this pittance out of fear and shame. We don't believe that another man could come and love us fully and we fear making the mistake of allowing a pedophile or otherwise abusive man into our child's life so we settle into the bullshit dynamic with the biological father in an effort to give our children a complete experience as well as stave off loneliness in our own love lives. You are worth more than the fruit of your genitals. You are more than your mistakes.

Many single mothers have gone on to lead extraordinary lives, accumulating impressive educational and vocational resumes, starting businesses, raising phenomenal children, and yes, even getting married and building or rebuilding nuclear families with wonderful men. Any or all of those possibilities are open to you too but not if you keep holding on to a situation that's been long dead. Freedom starts with choice, or more specifically the acknowledgement of the choices you have. When you say "he won't leave me alone" you're putting all the cards in his hands.

Of course he won't! Why would he when he gets everything for nothing? Only a saint or a fool would walk away from unlimited access to the world's greatest treasure with no responsibility on his behalf. This isn't about playing hard to get, this is about understanding that *he's not even qualified to have you in the first place*. The fact that you allowed him access to you once should not be a lifetime sentence to make the same mistake in perpetuity. One of my go-to sayings is *I can show you better than I can tell you*.

Talk is and always has been cheap. You've been threatening him for as long as you've been talking to him and he clearly doesn't believe you. He's not wrong. You wouldn't be here if any of the things you told him about your standards and what you would and wouldn't put up with were true. We put more value on the existence of the relationship than the **quality** of the relationship. How can you be in love with someone you fundamentally do not, and **can** not trust? Continuously placing an untrustworthy person in a seat of power in your life begins to eat away at your trust in *yourself* and that is the key to your downfall. The cornerstone of self-esteem is trust in ones self over time, and once that's gone self-hatred is sure to take its place.

People love to say "God knows my heart". Well your subconscious does too, and best believe it's keeping score. Stop playing victim and get him out of your life. If he's not paying bills, actively helping to rear his children, or just generally adding to a sense of the stability and peace in the household he needs to go. Stop hiding behind technicalities. *"Oh we were on a break, we're not together, we are co-parenting"* ... Eye roll. The saying goes that people in glass houses shouldn't throw stones. Well, I say that drama is throwing stones from inside of your glass house and then wondering why you're homeless, your feet are bleeding, and there's glass in your eye.

I'm speaking to women because I am not a man and I cannot speak from a man's perspective to be able to give advice to men about what they should do. Understand that I do not feel like the sole responsibility is with the woman. That being said, you must ask yourself this question: do I respect him? Respect is a key component to any successful male/ female relationship. Both men and women tend to think that is less important to have respect from the man towards the woman as it is to have from the woman towards the man. I have my own opinions about that but for now I will focus on respect towards the man.

It is a commonly known fact that men require respect from their significant other in order to bond with them emotionally.

LEVEL ⬆*P*

It is my opinion that the major problem between men and women in this society is the woman's ignorance or dismissal of their lack of respect for their man. This lack of respect may be warranted, but like I said it is the death of intimacy between the two parties. If you find that you lack respect for your baby's father but still wish to be with him you're fighting an uphill battle.

If you cannot find something in this person to respect it will be like salting the Earth and nothing good or useful will ever grow from your interactions. it should go without saying at this point that if you cannot find something to respect in this person there is no reason to continue this relationship. You're just wasting time. No one can lie to you SUCCESSFULLY without you first lying to yourself. Other people's Bullshit is ineffective unless your defenses have first been weakened by your own.

LEVEL U̸P

LEVELING UP

We always talk about "real recognizing real" and not tolerating fake-ness from other people, but what do you do when the snake in your life tearing you down is YOU? The one holding you back from pursuing your dreams is YOU? The one keeping you surrounded by negative influences is YOU? The one keeping you too distracted and exhausted to accomplish your goals is YOU? YOU are NOT to be trusted and your higher self knows it.

Think about the moments when you're snapping at your kid(s) while in your own head you are wondering why you are so mad at this little person that you love SO much and how the things flying out of your mouth at them are so horrible, yet you can't seem to stop. If you're constantly at a level of 45 on a scale from 1-10, if you are increasingly resentful of the multitude of tasks that make up your list of daily responsibilities pertaining to your child(ren), if you're constantly looking to the past or future and unable to sit still and quiet in the HERE and NOW and feel joyful without feeling like or fearing that it's just temporary, you are most certainly not happy and I can guarantee that it is affecting your relationship to and with your child(ren) even if you think you're holding it together. No matter how much you spend on extravagant clothes, toys, or trips, if you do not proactively

69

deal with the negative feelings that you harbor about the harsher realities of your situation they WILL manifest in the form of mood swings, risky and or overindulgent behavior, and an unhealthy to the point of obsessive need to try to control people and situations that aren't, never were, and never will be in your control.

We have all been and seen this single mother before. She can be a combination of any or all of these characteristics:

Combative

- against anyone giving her/her children CONSTRUCTIVE criticism or WARRANTED correction

Aggressive

- towards anyone and everyone including her children
- short tempered

Permissive

- allowing her children to run all over her and anyone unlucky enough to be in their vicinity
- Allowing men to use and abuse her/her children

Neglectful

Of her children:

- not attending to their needs in the most basic of ways (feeding, bathing, properly clothing them, etc.)

- not monitoring and establishing standards for academic performance and behavior
- spending all her free time with men or in the streets

Of Herself:

- not keeping herself reasonably presentable
- isolating herself and or her children unnecessarily
- limiting her own options due to a sense of duty and or hopelessness

Over Indulgent

Of The Child(ren):

- by having lax or nonexistent standards of behavior
- flimsy boundaries or none at all
- no real consequences for poor behavior
- Spending obscene amounts of money on material things

Of Herself:

- using food , alcohol, sex , drugs, social media, relationships, etc. as a stand in for self esteem, to numb unwanted emotions, block bad memories, compensate for un met expectations, and replace the things they really want but don't believe they can have for whatever reason

It is important that you understand that having real HUMAN feelings and reactions doesn't make you a bad person. Nor does it make you a bad mother. To the contrary, taking ownership of the real and valid feelings of regret and remorse that you may have surrounding how you became a mother and the subsequent realities of your day to day experience will not only help you be a better and less volatile mother, it will help you to be a more centered and secure PERSON. The kind of person who focuses on what is possible instead on what they should've, could've, or would've done. The kind of person who wins at life.

In the beginning of this book I cited Ciara as the perfect example of what we all strive for. While she is the beneficiary of resources far beyond our own the blueprint is not so much in what she has but in **how she uses** what she has. Ciara didn't spend her time stalking Future, fighting with his (innumerable) girlfriends and subsequent baby's mothers, or playing herself once she realized he was not about to settle down with her and their son. She kept it moving! She focused on her baby and her career. And, she reaffirmed her belief in her value as a woman.

If were being honest, she had taken her fair share of L's when it came to dating. She seemed to have had the misfortune of being used and discarded a time or two, same as the rest of us, all while in the public eye. She had to have been embarrassed and angry about the way things went down. How was she able to transition so gracefully from one man's discarded baby's mother to another's treasured wife? I know what she wasn't doing: limiting herself by believing that Future was the only man in this world worth having. She also wasn't spending her time trying to orchestrate events that would force him in to being with her on her terms.

As I mentioned earlier, trying to suppress anger and hurt about our situation can cause us to unintentionally redirect that same energy towards things and people we don't mean to. It can also cause us to fixate on those we deem responsible for our pain and as a result focus on them by trying to teach, coerce or punish them instead of feeding the more positive connections in our lives. Energy doesn't dissipate. It is either held, transferred or transformed. Holding on to negative energy keeps you from truly enjoying the fruits of your life. Transferring negative energy starts and perpetuates a continuous cycle of drama and conflict. The best option is to transform the bad feelings by working through them and releasing the condemnation and judgement they are accompanied by.

Ciara, along with other celebrities like Nicole Ari Parker have spoken of a "prayer" that seemed to conjure up the presence of their current husbands. Men who are just as desirable mentally and emotionally as they are aesthetically. While they both have explained the types of things they requested in their partners I've noticed that the most important component of what they said is continuously overlooked. They both went on to say that after praying for their husbands to come they PREPARED THEMSELVES to receive them! They didn't just pray to be given what they wanted, they prayed for guidance to become available and worthy of the blessings they asked for.

They used the time between making the request and receiving it to become who THEY needed to be. If the circumstances we find ourselves in are a direct result of who we have been to this point wouldn't it make sense that we need to change in order to experience something different? This should be especially apparent to those of us with multiple baby's fathers. Ciara learned the lesson life is trying to teach us. She learned that in order to have you must first *become*.

So how do you tackle this area of the process?

1. LET GO OF NEGATIVITY
   - Feel the hurt, but don't become it.
   - Show yourself compassion and forgive yourself for your mistakes whenever the harsh feelings surface.
   - Make amends for the ways you've neglected yourself. Rinse and repeat as needed.
2. BE ACCOUNTABLE
   - Take responsibility for the parts you play in your downfalls.

- Take stock of your weak points and prepare accordingly.
- Nobody knows you like you so if you know something is a slippery slope for you don't climb that particular mountain in the first place. Compassion doesn't equal complacency.
- Evaluate outside criticism before dismissing it. Be open to correction. Take the parts that ring true to heart (no matter who it comes from) and forget the rest
- Allow yourself to relax and feel good without getting carried away and abandoning your common sense.

3. GET BUSY
    - Whatever you've been putting off due to lack of confidence or support, DO IT! Fitness goals? DO IT! Creative ideas? DO IT! Now is the time to give life to whatever POSITIVELY CHARGED desires have been buried beneath the chaos of your clouded judgement and misdirected energy. If money is an issue than work on finding out how to raise the money you need. If you've already begun your endeavor prior to deciding to leave him alone enjoy the benefit of not having that weight on your back any longer.

4. BE BLESSED

- Wish your BF well, authentically. Still do whatever you need to for your child's benefit, but do so with pure intentions.
- Dance, sing, play and be silly.
- Spend time with yourself. Really learn to cherish your own company.
- Love and Honor your body. Nourish, pamper, and adorn it. Done right, this feels so good that you'll be able to tell the difference when someone is just trying to use it.
- Remember that you deserve all the good this life has to offer no matter how you may have messed up in your past.

CONCLUSION

You should be proud of yourself for making it this far in your life no matter what you've done or not done. And after reading this I hope you are excited for what is to come. I know I'm excited for you! My intent behind this book is to let you know that you are not as alone as you may feel and that you are and have always been valuable. Despite any and every person in your past that treated you otherwise.

I just saw a video the other day of a four year old baby matter of fact-ly saying she was ugly while looking at herself in the camera. It could only have been her subconscious speaking through her, the way it rolled right off her tongue. She didn't even seem bothered by it. It wasn't until the adult caring for her in that moment corrected her and began to speak affirmations of her beauty and value to her that she broke down, sobbing from deep within her little brown body. If a four year old baby can be carrying around that much self loathing after not possibly being able to have done anything to warrant feeling so imagine what you've been carrying inside you.

I want you, no, I *need* you to understand that any value you command in this world originates from within *YOU*. I'm not a religious person but I do read the bible from time to time and one of my favorite verses is "Cast not Ye Pearls before Swine".

LEVEL UP

While it can be fun to think of the people who hurt or reject us as "swine", I take this verse to mean that not everyone will understand the value of what it is that you have to offer and so you shouldn't keep trying to give it to them because they won't treat it properly. They don't have the capacity to understand anymore than a pig would understand the value of a pearl. They just don't have the range.

I don't know about you, but for me that takes some of the sting out of being rejected. It also helps me to understand that my value is still viable even if someone else doesn't see it. Believe in your own value so that you can teach your babies how to believe in theirs. Whatever you wish for them strive to create for yourself first. Even if you don't quite make it you will instill in your child(ren) an invaluable life skillset. Even more importantly though, do it for **YOU** Sis, because **You deserve to be Happy**.

www.ingramcontent.com/pod-product-compliance
Lightning Source LLC
Chambersburg PA
CBHW041358090426
42741CB00001B/6